Heart / Land

POEMS OF
LOVE & LANDSCAPE

Michael Gilkes

authorHOUSE®

AuthorHouse™
1663 Liberty Drive
Bloomington, IN 47403
www.authorhouse.com
Phone: 1 (800) 839-8640

Published by AuthorHouse 09/11/2015

ISBN: 978-1-5049-4781-7 (sc)
ISBN: 978-1-5049-4780-0 (e)

Contents

Acknowledgements

"the following poems have appeared previously in 'Joanstown and other poems' published by Peepal Tree Press Ltd. 17 King's avenue LS6IQS, Leeds, England:

'Swimmer', 'Morne Fortune', 'the Hook', 'Saint Lucy', 'Late Sonnet'.

The poems 'Returnee' and 'Fall' were previously published in *The Arts Journal (48 Eping Avenue, Bel Air Park, Georgetown, Guyana)*

Diamond Gilkes

Dawn light in the forest's high canopy of leaves
filters down sketching in branches and trunks of trees.
Below, a creek glistens. A corial heading for the river
leaves a trail of white lace in the V of its wake.
Water falling from paddles sparkles like diamonds.
Mist clouds the river, hiding its secret life.
Outboard engine roaring, the corial slices
the water like a knife.

A small neat figure sits bolt upright
in the dead centre of the boat. Two Amerindians
one at the prow a lookout for rocks and tacouba
the other in the stern steadying the rudder.
Above the engine's roar a harsh screeching.
Blue and red macaws flying in formation overhead.
Hanon Anon buttons his cotton sack coat
against the cold. Derby, cravat and walking stick
match his Victorian Saracen blade moustache.
He swivels his head from bank to bank as the mist clears.
His eyes miss nothing. A Kingfisher hurtles past
swift and silent as a feathered blowpipe dart.
Halfway up a tree in a mahogany stand
a three-toed sloth climbs slow-motion hand over hand.

Diamond-seeking following rivers and trails
had been the love of Hanon Anon's life.
It separated him from Town and wife.
His love was the Interior. "He bury there"
an old Amerindian said, "at San San Kopai"
a name meaning 'without a hope in hell'.
It was a Landing on the Putareng
not yet on any map. Hanon had made
a sketch of the location which he kept

for safety in the weathered, oil-black Bible
that he travelled with when time came to go.
He knew the river well. There his love
of the Interior began. He found diamonds
built a great wooden house in town
gave his elder daughter a stylish wedding.
The carriage horses' reins were diamond-studded
diamonds glistened like her own bright tears
upon her wedding gown made of fine silks.
It was Talk of the Town for many years.
Hanon Anon became Diamond Gilkes.

Perhaps the double 'Anon' was a black hole
that diamonds could not fill, that left him nameless,
faceless, without a home. He was alone
except when traveling, exploring the Interior he loved.
There he lived with trees, rivers, mountains,
waterfalls. The lure that drove him on
was heaven-sent for it was Nature herself,
and, like the great forests, needed no name.
One day all the diamonds were gone, spent
on things to help and please family and friends.
He packed his gear and Bible to go away once more
into that Interior world that made him whole.
It was the final harbour of his restless soul.
There is no headstone. There is no grave.
But bless you, grandfather, like mother nature
everything you had you gave.

Note:
'Hanon Anon' actually are the Christian names of the author's grandfather.
'Diamond Gilkes' (his nickname) was, with a partner named Kaufmann, the first
person in Guyana to mine diamonds commercially. He died during his last visit
to the Interior and was buried in an unmarked grave on San San Kopai island
on the Putareng river.

Permission to Land

The Piper Cub's high-pitched whine was the only sound.
Sea of blue above us, ocean of green below. Around
us and ahead fifty shades of green. The canopy on show.
Our pilot recounted rougher flights: an attempt at mirth
too casual for comfort, I thought,
caught as we were between blue heaven and green earth.
Then the rivers appeared: necklaces finely wrought
by a master silversmith. They curled delicately and shone
like the iguana's jewelled skin, linking the forest's greens
their sheen smudged by the aircraft's shadow in the sun.
Our shadow-plane took on the shapes of valleys and hills:
elongated, shortened as it slid over canopy and creeks
until humped mountains appeared. They raised their heads above
broad shoulders and began turning towards us as if to speak
then settling down again. The pilot waved a hand
shouting "You see those mountains? Those are the Kanukus, man !"
Our plane began its slow descent.
We had received permission to land.

Seawall

In boyhood we learned to swim in mud. Coffee-coloured Wireless pool,
'forty foot' canal aback the Botanical Gardens
even Punt Trench in spite of snakes and slippery banks.
But seawall swimming was first choice. That milk chocolate
water's gentle waves made it easy to float or swim.
Mud and sediment buoyed us up. Salt in that water didn't sting.
One day my father took me with him to join his friends
for a swim at the seawall. My first swim in the company of men.
Between the 'Shelter Belt' and 'Groyne', between river and sea
there was something very odd.
The sea was almost blue, clear, a line of white foam
running across straight as a surveyor's rod.
Orinoco's mouth was shut. Mud and silt had disappeared.
It looked like a mirage. Then, laughing, my father and friends
ran into it calling me to join them men and boy
all scooping up handfuls of mint blue water
like pork-knockers who had discovered gold.
That day the sea-walled ocean had let us behold
its hidden face. After that day no matter how old I grew
Nature would never again be what I thought I knew.

Mother / Nature

He couldn't remember when or how he'd won
the scholarship. Now he was a College boy.
From now on he would have to take the bites:
the mosquito nets were gone. He was to find
a world full of mosquitos, blood-suckers
whose stings would soon destroy his peace of mind.
He caught malaria from their bites and spent
each weekend shivering with fever in his bed
for one whole year. His mother found relief for him
in succulent weeds that grew in muddy corners
underneath the house. She knew them all.
Kunga Pump, Dill, Soldier Parsley, Amaranth.
She made warm teas with them, hot broths
that drove the fever out and eased the pain
of ague and fatigue.
Mother / Nature had come to his aid.

He decided to arm himself against future attacks
with weapons found in Nature. The golden apple's
hidden spikes the nutmeg's tough corselet of mace
the pineapple's plumed Molotov Cocktail
the scimitars and sponges of the stinking-toe tree
the yellow trumpets of the Morning Glory
the coconut's green helmets the lances
of the brushstroke-leafed bamboo
the rough and rusty armour of the tamarind.
His battle cry would be the music of the forest.
The spiraling scales of the Arapaima
the Bell bird's maddening arpeggios
the flugel horn of the struck trumpet tree
the Musician Wren's melodic warning call.
To build up his strength he would go to Nature.
He learned to drink the starapple's tart milk

And to avoid the sapodilla's slant black eyes
when tasting its quivering brown flesh.
He ate all the mangoes he could eat:
july, maidenhair, long mango, Buxton spice.
He cut squares from the pawpaw's sweet meat
and ate them from the teflon dinner plates
of lotus leaves culled from roadside canals.
On kiskadee mornings, when the flambouyante's
green fingers open like a sensitive plant
he would sing loud his praises to the most high
eucalyptus trees, wind turning the torn parchment of their bark
like pages of the book of Nature that had been
his Mother and his guide.

Swimmer

Everything he did came easily.
Trees dropped their fruit
for him to catch.
Fires lit for him
with one damp match.
Rain filled his bucket to the brim.
The yard, the circles
of cousins, friends,
the childhood games,
the gabled house
familiar as its housemaids' names
buoyed his young life
so he could swim.

In those green days
boyhood meandered
like a creek
finding its course,
changing its mind.
He wanted to leave the source behind,
go where the sun's glow lit the river's rim
making the forest cyclorama dim
to gold.
He longed to sing with tongues of Gauldings
blown like white confetti across the evening's scrim.
He longed to skim that changing surface
dimpled as a dinner gong.
Older swimmers said 'boy you too young.
That water deep. The currents-dem too strong.'
So life went on. The river pursued its course.

One day, years later, it called to him.
He heard its song.
Its voice was hoarse.
Raucous as sin.
Its amber face reflected his as he slipped in,
his body a bateau unzipping the dark water's skin.
Later, half drowned, glug-glugging on a Coke,
sucking a cigarette,
he'd watched as his struck match ignited the dusk
exploding with a flash of scarlet Ibises into sunset.
Towelled and dry his skin smelt of the river's musk.
Swimmer, he knew that smell would stay for good
like a dark, carcinogenic stain.
Nothing in life would come easy again.

The White Box

The visitor who said it was 'a big white box' was right.
He'd looked at the building with jaded, tourist's eyes. He saw
no dreaming spires, no carved and fluted stone, just a white
wooden box, so plain, so simple a child could draw
it. Seen in perspective, (say from the penthouse roof of the National Bank),
the Cathedral becomes a thing of beauty: the symmetry
of that vaulting wood, the arched doorways, the daring slant
of its spare, gleaming, galvanized roofs avoid the mimicry
of those great domed, turreted cathedrals. How could he know
that this was made, set down to be a city's centerpiece :
that from that central font so many rivers flow
to bless our landscape ? (those great pouring waterfalls will never cease
their fountaining) That water, like this font's, makes us all raceless. W<u>hole</u>.
Go in. Sit down. Let its still centre enter your soul.

Note:
The Anglican Cathedral, which still stands overlooking the city of Georgetown,
Guyana, is the largest and tallest wooden building in the world.

Five toad poems

1. Toad song

On country roads in pale moonlight
crapauds croak at dead of night.
And when their croaking stops you've felt the fright
take hold. Within that hush someone will die tonight.
They say when toads abort their chorus
that sudden silence is for the dead, not for us.
Call it superstition, for so it seems;
but pray no toads croak in your dreams.

2. Cane Toad

Once upon a time
I was an African prince. Here, I'm *Bufo Marinus*
buffoon of the sea, a drunken sailor. My skin isn't
corrosive, as experts think, though I confess
I like spraying my milk on pests who bother me.
Their eyes turn to ashpits with the burning.
That's why they keep me in this canefield. I guess
I'm a slave, but not to cut cane : to kill vermin.
I'll be free one day and a prince again. It just takes a kiss.
I've checked the women : I need a princess
so I'm out of luck. Here all I can see
are slaves and toads like me.

3. Toads of Remorse

Gone the carefree days of plenty.
Hair lies scattered on his head.
Arthritic, rusty-kneed, past seventy,
each night he climbs into his bed
to let the cold, dumb sheets embrace him.
Numb lips frame that chill word "wife".
One day a casket will encase him.
Toads of remorse squat on his life.

4. Royal Toad

By night
In this enchanted wood
a jewelled toad comes down to drink
its own reflection
in the stream.
Bubbled eyes tender as love, reflect
the curvature of earth,
the moon's bright beam.
Its squat, humped body settles on a rock
to dream.

By day
the wattled toad becomes
a thing of dread.
Its slimy back and mottled head
are odious, obscene.
The Princess hurries from her bed
to rouse the sleeping Queen.
"Alas!. To know what I know!
To see what I have seen!"

5. Toad Map

The ancient maps of intrepid explorers were fashioned
meticulously. Works of Art, they gave the world
a wondrous display of cartographical design: the art of plunder
and of conquest underlay the skills those draughtsmen knew.
Observe the delicate lines of those wind-bellied sails, the fountaining
whales as consorts and the warnings to the reader ' here be dragons'
or 'here be men whose heads do grow beneath their shoulders.'
But if you look with a bold, indigenous eye under the great ships
the monsters belching water and fire the conquerors astride the world
You will see toads.

On Larkin's 'Aubade'

(for Jenny and Peter)

Larkin's 'Aubade' is the gloomiest poem you'll ever read.
His obsession with death is an addictive need.
No lasting, warm relationships, no loving wife,
a great toad of despair squats on his life.
There's nothing to be done, nothing to be said.
Nothing can shift that load of death inside his head.
Philip Larkin was an atheist, and though his argument is sound:
that death's 'the anaesthetic from which no one comes around'
that there's no thought, no light, no song
'nothing to think with,
nothing to love or link with'
beneath the language you can hear a longing to be proven wrong.

Jenny would have laughed, her eyes dancing though already weak.
She'd have heard that longing in Larkin's poetspeak.
and she would know, and Peter too, why Larkin chose that form
'aubade': a song of hope, of lovers welcoming the dawn.
Peter, and now Jenny, are gone. Our own evenings are coming on.
Their life together was an aubade to welcome love, laughter, song.
They've left us memories to think with
to love, and so, to link with.
A life, a death like theirs proves Larkin wrong.

Time for Poems

This is not a good time for poems.
Friends and lovers we have known are gone
forever, silently, leaving no turbulence in the air.
There's nothing to be said or to be done.
In passing they took everything, except those clear,
indelible lines they made in our minds, their poems.

This is not a good time for poems.
Nothing's left to build to lean on or to share.
The sand is a blank page left by a departing wave.
The ribbed beach has been stripped bare.
The sea has taken back all that it gave.
This is not a good time for poems.

And now another life begins its poem:
Antoinette Madree barely five pounds at birth.
Out of such small seeds great forests rise.
This daughter will grow stronger day by day, her eyes
deep as the brown rivers that water the earth.
She smiles.
This is a good time for poems.

Dog's love

We can learn the patience of dogs but not their love.
That love's too hard to learn, too unconditional.
Take this old terrier, his trust in me, his frank delight
at a bone-shaped biscuit thrown, so casually offered on my part :
the expectant look, a paw held out as if to claim the right
to nothing more than pleasure in my company.
There's no measuring the love in a dog's heart.
I'll miss him when he's gone
and wonder if there is a God who cares
and looks out for all dogs and sees me as I am,
throwing a bone-shaped biscuit to a dog named Sam :
a dog lover who believes whoever loves a dog loves God.

Loquats

From a distance they look like hog plums,
bright yellow skins drum-tight.
Up close they soon become
hypnotic, glowing orange-coloured light
bulbs each in the socket of a wire-hard stem.
Loquats, more gold than those "golden lamps
in a green night" of Marvell's mythic poem
'Bermudas', the utopian dream that stamps
on the mind an image of this magical island
transparent as its limpid lagoons, yet cloaked in mystery.
Unscrewing a loquat I plump it in my hand:
sweet/sour fruit of myth and island history.

Food chain

The blackbird was a damn nuisance.
It kept flying in, bold as you please, to pick
the crumbs right off my plate, keeping itself
just out of reach, eyeing my first meal of the day.
It couldn't wait for me to leave, flaunting itself,
the little thief. To drive it away
I threw a fork and then a teaspoon at it,
missed, knocking a teacup to the floor.
The bird retreated, checked the broken shards
for food and then flew off.
Sure enough it soon came back to taunt me,
always just out of reach, bright, yellow eyes like beads.
Finally I hit it with a well-aimed wad of bread
kneaded into a ball. A small blizzard of feathers
and the bird, its eyes still bright as beads,
lay dead.
I'd only meant to scare, not kill the thing.
Now those beady yellow eyes would haunt me.
Ashamed, wanting it out of range
of sight or feeling, my breakfast ruined,
I held it by the black twigs of its feet
and flung it out into the street.
A cat, nothing but ribs and filthy mange,
appeared like magic out of nowhere, gently
sniffed the tiny corpse, then settled down
to its first meal of the day.
Nature wastes nothing.

'Colly'

The brown, unruly hair has been brushed back
by a hand busy with its newest book.
The verandah's sea-grape leaves filter the light
lending the generous features a sepia look.
Proclaim him intellectual and white,
but look behind that actor-teacher's stance:
you'll see a casual Bajan in short pants,
barefooted, in a rocking chair that's older
than his years. One foot is planted on the ground,
the other keeps the rhythm of the rocking chair
turning the pages of the sea. 'I must always
be remembering the sea' he writes with a grin.
The words become sandpipers' arrows on wet sand
pointing the way into the castle of his skin.

Farine

"When they ask me to what *angst* I owe my art I tell them
it's the farine. Not bad, eh? For a poor black boy
from Chaussée road, Castries"
The head is weathered rock. He sits, a rock on the beach
of his verandah. He laughs, a wave breaking on rock,
rough granite opening to unexpected crystal.
"So how you find the pear"? More laughter. The joke's on me.
wielding a large fork like a palette knife, he
crushes peeled halves of fresh avocado
into a mound of farine. Now the fork's a sable
blending colours in the enamelled palette-bowl on the table.
Some more pastel-yellow avocado. A drizzle
of olive oil to darken and give an ochre glow
to the farine. Curled wedges of lime, like squeezed tubes,
lie on the table, their colour mirroring the irises
of those slow, yellow-green, mulatto eyes. The broad
Neanderthal forehead shines with the sweat of a Nobel Prize.
"It's the farine, but you have to get the mixture right."
For ab-originals and Nobel laureates
there is no *angst* in art or appetite.

Summit

Who are they?
All those wrinkled men in black, their wrinkle-proof suits
fit only for funerals
or weddings of the rich and famous. The destitute
stand bootless under black trees on baked earth
waiting for rain
for help that comes always too late
and brings no water
if it comes at all.
Only more men in black, the Councils they are holding
like dung beetles rolling the world's frail wealth
into a concrete ball
they call the Developed World. It is a world
of their own making.
It too will fall.

Lycanthrope

Well, he was artistic. The attentive kind
that women liked. Good looker, handsome
but not vain. Even a hooker might dream to find
a man like that. He would take time. Not come
and go. But, they said, he was so often away.
And why he went, and to what distant places
no one knew. Some thought perhaps he might be gay:
an actor, sensitive, a man of many faces.
At night he lived another life inside his head.
He walked alone, wolflike, the darkness clear as light,
loping along dark alleyways of lust and dread
seeking the hunter's pleasure at the sight
of unsuspecting victims, their warm blood
calling to him until he felt his own blood shake,
the stony earth on which he stood
becoming pliant under his paws, the ache
of canine teeth emerging through muscled jaws:
bright metal spikes designed to tear and break.
His parched tongue would drink deep tonight.
By day he was again the handsome stranger with the ready smile
everyone liked. The wolf within stayed out of sight,
incisors now retracted from the light.

Stalker

You were on my trail before I knew that I
was destined from the start to be your prey.
When you whispered that the vaulted sky
was empty and that even friends betray
I prayed that flame burning inside my breast
might one day become a blazing sun
outlasting destiny, friendship and all the rest
until the spinning earth had ceased to run.
You stalked me while I worked, when I drew breath,
entering at last my chambered heart, your breath
coming and going, painfully, like my breath.
Now, as darkness falls and shadows stalk the land
I write this sonnet with a steady hand.
My poetry will live. I do not fear you, Death.

(developed by request from a draft by Ronald Lightbourne)

Surveyors

He'd seen the 1997 Tourist Board print.
Brochure-blue Bermuda sky, cerulean sea, pink sand.
This was its negative, a transparency of the island
in 1797, etched like an aquatint.
One filmed from the sky the other plotted by hand
from a leaky boat with plumb lines and staves.
A survey for Master Hurd by two of his slaves.
It looked like a high-tech ultrasound scan
of a womb, curled foetus resting circled
by its amniotic, grey sea.
Held up to the light it began to look
like the inside of a stomach with a fish hook,
swallowed, that has come to rest lying
in wait to be the reason for the swallower's dying.

Leaf

There's no knowing which final stone or snowflake
starts the avalanche. Everywhere seductions
of stability and power assure us it won't happen.
Hiroshima, Chernobyl, Fukushima
taught us nothing. Hearts are hard as stone.
Neither victim nor aggressor
nor a hundredweight of Catholic bells
can reach the human heart's dry, stony ground.
A leaf falls from the forest canopy without a sound.

Fall

I dream of a waterfall
an amber torrent sliding silent
over rough lips and teeth of stone.
Down in the gorge below, the rainbow mist:
a bridal veil marrying water rock and sky.

I am standing on a tongue of rock
too close to the fall
as in that photograph of my son Kai
standing there where no one ought to stand
unless to die.

I am naked, without fear, hearing the roar
of water that can wear all rocks away, feeling
that pull, that old longing to fly
up, up and up to be for evermore
wedded to elemental water, rock and sky.

Sun

Sun is a dragonish sky god belching fire
as all benighted peoples knew.
Our modern hi-tech telescopes with higher
resolution now confirm their view.

Shaman

His death shall be a stone thrown into a creek
breaking the water's mirror leaving no trace
burying itself in mud. The ripples will seek
the far banks of the dreaming rivers of space.

Writer

(for Angela)

A woman, the grey in her hair just beginning,
sits at her desk in a modest pink house
made of traditional Bermuda white coral.
She writes with a black marker on a whiteboard
'Bermuda's history: a story of Beginning'.
The tetrameters roll on like the waves of the sea.
Words become breakers over submarine rocks
where once there were forests of towering cedars
and conch shells with barnacles older than the sea
older than legends older than history.
Longtails are circling their nests in the rocks.
A great storm is coming. The darkening sky
is heavy with cloud. Tank rain sings loud
in the veins of the house. The waves grow higher.
Liquid mountains are rising in the air.
The salt from their spume flies in the wind
and the smell of the sea is everywhere.
Hurricane winds are devils howling
at the end of the world and chaos beginning...
The writer erases the words on the board and writes
'Genesis.'

Blue

In this new, blue garden chair (a modern
upright version of the Berbice chairs I knew
in my Guyana childhood) I take my ease
sliding into its blue. This chair has
no carved holes for the glass of rum fetched
for the sprawling, booted master by his slaves. This blue
blends with the garden's green. A rose pink house
completes your scenic Bermuda colours. Blue sea
pink sand and green, green everywhere you look.
But in this hook-shaped atoll there are blues
of everlasting beauty and of pain.
There are no masters now, no slaves,
but this chair's ease connects a slave uprising
with your ordered, quiet and quiescent
island life. The chains that link Benin,
Bermuda and Berbice remain within.
And In Guyana once, walking in deep forest
in fading light, unsure of the way through,
ahead of us Morphos had suddenly appeared
flashing like beacons their incandescent blue.

Heart / land

"Islands can only exist if we have loved in them."
(Derek Walcott)

Awake in his hospital bed he rakes the sand
of memory for shards of his life's shipwreck:
bright baubles on the shore of that fabled island
where once he stood secure on a rock- hard deck
suspended above an azure sea.
A blur of faces. The anthem soaring.
A sprinkle of rain, the clink of glasses,
the tinkle of a fallen ring, rolling...
In the darkness the flash of torchlight beams.
Night nurse patrolling.
He closes his eyes and sees
shafts of dawn-light filtering
through the forest canopy like mist or rain
a Red Howlers'chorus rising and falling
the woman asleep, fitful, recalling
the naked power of the forest's embrace,
giant greenheart bedposts towering
above the canopy's spidery lace
of mosquito netting, lianas thick as anacondas
sliding over leaf-choked rivulets with no end or beginning.
She knew she must leave to set herself free
from meandering creeks, inscrutable brown rivers
to return to horizons of clear, blue sea.

Her leaving was painful: a greenheart splinter lodged
in his mind. It would grow toxic as time went on.
The poison was already at work. She was gone.
He turns on his side to ease the pain.
The splinter burns. Never. Never. Never. Never.
Never to see her again!

It would be as if the island and everything in it
vanished under those reefs of clouds that had parted
as the plane came in and he saw for the first time
the chalk-white roofs, the baize-covered golf courses clipped
and clean and ridiculously green and the indigo Sound
winged with white sails of skiffs as stiff and proud
as swans on an English pond.
A paradise where prim hedges are kept
meticulously trimmed
and the flawless pink beaches
daily brushed and swept.
Where In May roadside hedges show
scarlet cherries and Loquat trees glow
with bright orange lanterns. Rosemary and fennel grow
wild as weeds and bermudianas start springing
from unlikely places like a beautiful song
even hurricanes cannot silence for long.

But the island was shaped like a hook, a pseudo-atoll:
every tempest-tossed shipwreck's final landfall.
Island and woman would begin to seem
like nothing more than a waking dream.
A miracle that comes only once in a lifetime:
a space warp
that opens once in a hundred years and will close again
with a snap
as soon as the woman who caused that time-shift
no longer wanted his love nor could give hers to him
for islands can only exist when we love in them.
That would be the signal for gathering clouds
to cover the island for another hundred years
until another woman from that magical land
broke its law and fell in love again with a man
from that forested world full of uncertainties
beyond the reach of her dreaming islands
and the certainties found only there in that Erewhon

seen as mirages are seen, a mere trick of the sun.
Those explorers who find it are able to do so
only by the enchantment that loving a woman
from that island can bring. If that love should fade, so
would the island and everything in it. And then it would seem,
he imagined, as if a hundred years had passed like the shadow
of a cloud and at last he beheld the truth,
for now he was old. His youth had deserted him
and all he had left were regret and longing.

His body felt cold
as if a cool wind
had suddenly strolled in
at its own sweet will
through the open window
beside his bed.
He pulled the blanket
up over his head
but he still felt cold.

He awoke to a childhood chorus of kiskadees
piercing the morning air and splayed fingers
of palmetto fans, like batons, conducting the breeze.
The palmettos were Bermudian.
The birds were Guyanese.
He looked at the sky now gold in the sun.
Island and Heartland were one.

Song for Rima

You can tell sun's in her blood
and all the seasons. Spring, Winter,
Summer's flood,
the Autumn colours that still tint her
hair. In that green island she would grow
straight as a tasseled, flowering cane arrow.
Wherever home was, whatever its setting,
she would make it hers.
And always there was love and no regretting
what might have been for better or for worse.
What **was** was always enough :
the cobalt sea, the casuarinas singing in a seasonless landscape.

Even when the sea change came and, yes, it was tough
waking to find the accustomed shape
of things altered, no windows framing the sky's blue scrim,
no casuarinas singing, a sea too cold to swim,
her spirit never faltered. She found room to run
in fields and wooded hills down to this new island's rim.
Now life had to be charted: the fun
of living had to be earned,
dots had to be connected, new rules lived by.

But then, since childhood, she had learned
to connect the dots of stars in the night sky,
to feel the sun's authority on her skin until it burned.
Nature and human nature shaped her from inside:
her mother's love a rock, her father's like the tide
forever leaving and returning, wanting nothing but her good.
Her life is balanced now in the shared radiance of bride
and groom. Looking at them you can tell sun's in their blood.

Orphic lament

Without you
breakfast's just not worth the taking.
I've learned to give it a miss.
I drink black coffee instead, without you, at six,
my usual breakfast time before you came making
timetables tumble, then righting the world with a kiss.
Lunchtime's another quick coffee fix
and dinner's a sad business without you.
Last night, absent-mindedly, I set the table for two;
and once, I swear, I turned to look thinking I heard you
there appearing as only you can appear, beamed down from space.
Everything seems empty without you
though everything's in place
except a vase of flowers on the dining table
your music
and the scent of you.

Returnee

The mosquitoes are thinner and have learned not to whine.
Coastlanders still dream of flight to the interior.
Our muddy Atlantic's wavy boundary line
still divides us from blue waters by the murkier
design of Orinoco's continental reach.
The coastland's silken chocolate skin is scored
by Indian fishermen sliding across the beach :
mudskippers on a crude box-wood skateboard.
A black derelict, naked, squats in the street, huge
flaccid penis signalling manhood and its defeat.
The pavement vendors' barricades give refuge
only to the dispossessed, the weak.

At school, black Ravi Boodhoo with four
o's and only one eye, was unique.
His wound was tragic, like Oedipus's roar
of grief, a black hole of Calcutta. Now, as I speak,
such wounds are commonplace. No sight is whole.
I watch the moon climb through dark clouds like a thief
burning a dark circle in each cloud, a black hole
like the bullet-ant's signature on a giant palm leaf.

All fall down

Do not believe that this is how it ends :
a light-bulb switched off with a casual click,
a diver surfacing caught in the bends,
swift needles in the blood rushing to prick
and burst the swollen bubble of his heart.
No. A slip in the bath, the slow stumbling
of age, a fall tearing old sinews apart,
pain unfocusing the mind, the numbing
fear within: fear in blood and bone.
So it begins. Then pain and pain and pain alone.
I know. I stumbled once, badly, and fell.
But that was long before this load of pain.
Any fool who's had a fall knows well
the worst won't come until he's fallen again and again.

Braids

It was their first meal together; two strangers who
found love had chosen them in spite of time
and age and place. He lit the candle in the top
of an empty, oval-shaped, blue bottle of wine
celebrating their stolen hours. They talked non-stop,
their eyes bright as the rising, oval moon,
the candle melting as their love grew. She watched
his hands framing that wine bottle's peacock blue,
candle wax falling in braids of fine, white lace
as her mahogany braids would fall, undone,
framing the perfect oval of her face.
After that first meeting they both knew
the candle wax had braided a pattern time could not undo.
Their love would last in spite of time or age or place.

Morne Fortune

No man's an island (he'd read John Donne). His creative urge
sailed where the collective imagination sent.
He'd be like Harris's Dreamer, charting rivers of a continent
with a drowned crew, feeling that Atlantic surge.
When, upriver, his poetic craft got stuck
(that mud sucked men and poems down without a trace)
he figured island life might change his luck:
he'd seek the Antillean Genius of Place.

He managed to get a Creative Writer's grant
to live in Lucian hills, find a new slant.
"Bon bagai! My island *steep* in poetry, boy!"
encouraged a poet friend, St. Lucian born.
In Castries, boarding a mini-van, a sudden rush of joy.
The bearded driver was Triton blowing his wreathèd horn!
That sloe-eyed woman, Greek there, a black Helen of Troy!
The humped hills shouldering stars above the Morne
thrilled and intimidated him, like Wordsworth's Boy.
That night ride up Morne Fortune left him numb.
His continental brain, like a container lorry
grinding gears, changed into first.
At this height would his poems come
and stay until he'd winged them so they could glide down?
Tomorrow at dusk, his poem time, he'd know the worst.

From his high verandah dawn woke commonplace,
transparent as a housewife in her shift.
Trees in curlers, ravine breaking wind,
the hills still in their white mosquito nets of mist,
the valley smoking an early cigarette.
A light rain falling: the Morne washing its face.
It would take genius to make such flimsy stuff
reflect the Antillean Genius of Place.

The island, twinned by Laureate poetry to Greece,
still wasn't Greek. The cathedral chimes mimicked Big Ben.
No city sign sign said "Ithaca/Castries".
But if not Lucian landscape, well, what then?
At sundown, when he launched a trial poem,
the thing glided across the town and fell into the sea.
He was old Daedelus watching his son drown.

One day in town, hoping to find a poem or two
that he'd sent down, he dropped in for a beer
and stayed to listen to some poetry at the Rose & Crown.
The place was full of poets, one waxing eloquent
sipping a Piton (he'd sworn off Bounty for Lent),
swivelling his grey, unfocussed lion's eyes:
"You-all sit up here on your Pegasses;
You waiting in case fame or fortune calls?
Genius is jus' a man wif talent and
a bold attitude. You watch my smoke, gasson.
I take life by the balls, you know? Keep poetry
in my grip. O.K. big joke. I don't mean a suitcase.
Look. The Muse is a jablesse as you know well.
You have to take she so (grabbing the bottle)
and buss she mouth until you taste success.
You can't play noble and win a Nobel.
Gasson, you have to capay diem if you want
to write at all. Get off your high horse man!
You know? Pride goeth before a fall."

That sundown, back on Morne Fortune, he cried
to be unhorsed, envisioned, blinded, like Saul,
like Walcott, even like V.S. Naipaul.

Saint Lucy

Her name rings, with three long strokes,
the Benedictine convent's angelus.
Lampions are lit. The Vigie lighthouse turns, spokes
of light encircle the blind eyes of Saint Lucy. Benedictus.
The kneeling convent turns Its head to that light
like a girl, lips parted, tongue trembling for the Host,
for the sweet resinous wine of violons, as night
awakens the island's music. It comes up ghost-
like on the Morne: the kla-kla's song, the toutwelle's grieving,
the sad bellow of a lost cruiseliner, leaving,
and I an old man falling in love again.
That circling light, bright beyond believing,
returns. My words fly like moths to its flame
as the convent's angelus softly rehearses her name.

The Hook

Our silver fish-bellied aircraft takes off
tilting the island, its white roofs slanting dangerously,
until even the sea's blue slides away
slow-fading from cerulean blue to grey.
Munching a Bermuda chicken sandwich I peer
through the scratched plexiglass and feel, with a start,
as the clouds clear, the tug of that island's hook in my heart.

Breathing in that cold, thin air I'm pinned
squirming in my seat, out of my element,
back arched like the small bream young Sacha
dangled, wide-eyed, from the hook of an angler's line
baited with meat from a Bermuda chicken sandwich.

And though I should know that 'nothing gold can stay'
I want to remember forever that magical cay
where a boy's smile sparkled like the bright hull
of a boat with small fry leaping in its wake
like a handful of pebbles thrown or like white beads
of ocean spray, or like the flash of the fish he let go
to swim its way through the sun-sprinkled glittering water
of that beautiful bay.

A late sonnet

I've written this late sonnet to say something
my shaky voice could never say to you.
For poets past middle age, nothing
comes harder, believe me, than finding new
metaphors. Might as well try forging
steel without the fire to make it true.
Now it's trapped on paper, this awkward thing,
even the sentiment seems paper too;
the poem a dumb creature in its cage
unable to speak as I had meant it to.
If you could free this poem from its page
you'd understand my futile ague then;
that old malarial ache, that ancient rage
that makes old men of poets, poets of old men.

Printed in the United States
By Bookmasters